CITIES
LOS ANGELES

ABDO
Publishing Company

Nancy Furstinger

visit us at
www.abdopub.com

Published by ABDO Publishing Company, 4940 Viking Drive, Edina, Minnesota 55435.
Copyright © 2005 by Abdo Consulting Group, Inc. International copyrights reserved in all
countries. No part of this book may be reproduced in any form without written permission from
the publisher. The Checkerboard Library™ is a trademark and logo of ABDO Publishing Company.

Printed in the United States.

Cover Photo: Corbis
Interior Photos: Corbis pp. 1, 4, 5, 6-7, 8, 9, 10, 13, 14, 16-17, 18, 19, 20, 21, 22, 23, 25, 26, 27,
    28, 29; Getty Images pp. 12, 13, 15, 24

Series Coordinator: Jennifer R. Krueger
Editors: Megan M. Gunderson, Jennifer R. Krueger
Art Direction & Maps: Neil Klinepier

Library of Congress Cataloging-in-Publication Data

Furstinger, Nancy.
    Los Angeles / Nancy Furstinger.
        p. cm. -- (Cities)
    Includes index.
    ISBN 1-59197-861-0
    1. Los Angeles (Calif.)--Juvenile literature. I. Title.

F869.L84F87 2005
979.4'94--dc22
                                                                2004050850

CONTENTS

LOS ANGELES

The Los Angeles County coastline

In the 1700s, Spanish explorers were searching for places to build **missions**. In 1796, they came across a scenic river valley in what is now California. This beautiful area became the site of the City of Angels, or Los Angeles. Today, it is the second-largest city in the United States.

Los Angeles stretches across southwestern California. It is the largest city in the Golden State. The area is ringed by beaches, Pacific Ocean waves, the San Gabriel Mountains, and a tangle of freeways.

Today, the world sees Los Angeles as a center of entertainment and **culture**. It is a paradise for celebrities and celebrity watchers. But, its rich history extends far beyond that. It has grown from a small **pueblo** into a city that attracts residents and visitors from all over the world.

Angelenos can surf in the Pacific Ocean and ski in the San Gabriel Mountains in the same day!

LOS ANGELES AT A GLANCE

Date of Founding: 1781

Population: City: 3,694,820

County: 9,871,506

Metro Area: 466 square miles
(1,207 sq km)

Average Temperatures:
- 58° Fahrenheit (14°C) in cold season
- 70° Fahrenheit (21°C) in warm season

Annual Rainfall: 14 inches (36 cm)

Elevation: 275 feet (84 m)

Landmarks: La Brea Tar Pits,
Griffith Observatory,
Disneyland

Money: U.S. Dollar

Language: English

FUN FACTS

Santa Catalina Island is home to a herd of buffalo. They were brought to the island for a Zane Grey movie and set free to roam the island after filming!

Ground sloths, dire wolves, eagles, mammoths, mastodons, camels, bears, saber-toothed cats, and ancient bison are on view at the Page Museum at La Brea Tar Pits.

TIMELINE

1769 - Spanish explorers Gaspar de Portolá and Father Junípero Serra explore the Los Angeles River basin.

1781 - Governor Felipe de Neve and 14 families officially settle and name Los Angeles.

1821 - Mexico becomes independent from Spain.

1847 - What is now California is ceded to the United States.

1848 - The California gold rush brings more settlers to Los Angeles.

1850 - California becomes the thirty-first state.

1913 - Cecil B. DeMille begins filming movies in Hollywood.

1994 - A major earthquake collapses freeways and kills about 60 people.

2001 - James K. Hahn is elected mayor.

By establishing **missions**, Spain hoped to convert the Native Americans to Christianity. In 1769, Spain sent Gaspar de Portolá and Father Junípero Serra to explore California.

They built a trail of missions that stretched from San Francisco to San Diego.

The San Gabrielinos lived in the heart of what would become Los Angeles. These Native Americans were also called *Tongva*, or "People of the Earth." They ate plant foods, such as acorns and berries. They caught fish and wild game. Their homes were made from poles and woven grass.

Father Junípero Serra

Here in the Los Angeles River basin, Portolá and Father Juan Crespi met and traded with the San Gabrielinos. Three earthquakes shook the area during the Spanish explorers' visit. Still, they thought it would be the perfect place for a **pueblo**.

More than ten years later, Governor Felipe de Neve convinced 14 families to help him colonize the area. So in 1781, 44 people settled the site along the river. The settlers were mostly from northern Mexico. They named the site *El Pueblo de la Reyna de Los Angeles* or "The Town of the Queen of the Angels."

A statue of Father Junípero Serra stands outside the Mission San Gabriel Arcangel, which he founded in 1771.

The city's name was soon shortened to Los Angeles. By 1800, Los Angeles had 315 settlers. But, the sleepy **pueblo** was still under Spanish rule.

In 1821, Mexico became independent from Spain. So, what is now the state of California became part of Mexico's territory. After Mexico's rule ended in 1847, California was **ceded** to the United States.

Los Angeles city lights at night

In 1848, the gold rush brought more people to the area.

In 1850, California became the thirty-first state, and Los Angeles officially became a city. The new city numbered only 3,530 citizens. But by the time the city celebrated its one hundredth birthday, the population of Los Angeles was 11,000.

Today, the city of Los Angeles is home to nearly 4 million people. Los Angeles County contains more than 80 cities and nearly 10 million people. Los Angeles faces many problems common to large cities, including racial tensions and overcrowding. However, it remains a center for **culture** and the arts.

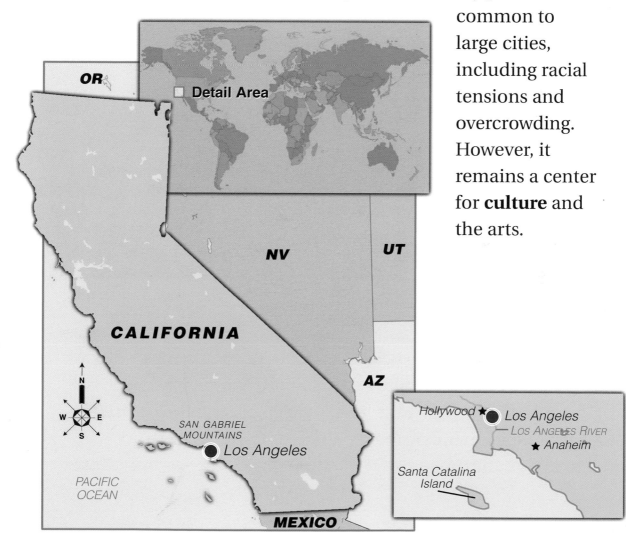

LEADERSHIP

The head of government in Los Angeles is the mayor. The mayor is elected to a four-year term. In 2001, Angelenos elected Mayor James K. Hahn. His major concerns are reducing crime, improving neighborhoods, and creating jobs and housing.

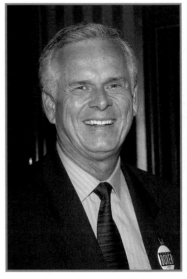

Mayor James K. Hahn

The mayor appoints several boards of **commissioners**. The commissioners help the mayor govern different programs in the city. The boards oversee the fire department, the city parks, and the transportation system.

The city of Los Angeles is divided into 15 districts. Every district is represented by a city council member. Each member is elected by the people living in his or her district. City council members serve four-year terms.

When it was completed in 1928, Los Angeles City Hall was the tallest building in the city.

TOM BRADLEY

In 1973, Tom Bradley became the first African-American mayor of a mostly white, major U.S. city. Bradley was a police officer and then a lawyer. After winning the race for mayor of Los Angeles in 1973, he went on to serve five terms!

In 1984, Bradley brought the Olympic Games to his city. They were a great success and earned a profit of $225 million. This was a reflection on his leadership as it was the first time the games had made money since 1932.

BUSY ROADS

One of the many busy intersections in Los Angeles

In 1928, city officials selected a tract of farmland to build an airport. Mines Field became Los Angeles Municipal Airport in 1930. In 1952, it became an international airport. By 1965, 10 million passengers had come to L.A. through the airport.

Once people arrive in L.A., they need to be able to move around easily. So, officials created the Metropolitan Transportation Authority (MTA). It helps make sure all forms of public transportation are safe and fast. The MTA is in charge of the bus system, the car pool and bike lanes, and the new rail system.

Even with this excellent public transportation system, most Angelenos drive their own cars. For this reason, Los Angeles is famous for its traffic problems. In 2001, the local government began a plan to improve conditions. Each year, the 25 worst intersections will be identified and put in line for improvements.

Los Angeles International Airport (LAX) is the fifth-busiest airport in the world. In 2003, more than 54.9 million travelers went through LAX.

Cattle and dairy farms, vineyards, and fruit orchards once surrounded Los Angeles. Today, freeways have replaced most of the farmland. But, Los Angeles still exports a variety of farm products, including plants, fruits, vegetables, and fish.

The city is also a leader in manufacturing. Angelenos make clothing, glass, jewelry, and oil-drilling machinery. Today's high demand for oil makes this machinery an important part of the city's **economy**. Electronics is a large industry in Los Angeles, too.

L.A. leads the world in producing aircraft. During **World War II**, the city began to build planes such as the B-1 bomber. Later, the industry expanded and built spacecraft for the Saturn, Apollo, and Voyager projects.

Besides manufacturing, Angelenos work in research, health, and banking. Tourism is also a top employer. And, filmmaking remains a leading industry.

The Port of Los Angeles is one of the busiest in the world.
Many industries use it to import and export products.

Cecil B. DeMille (left) and his crew on a film set in the early days of Hollywood

The motion picture business is one of the largest industries in Los Angeles. In 1913, director Cecil B. DeMille searched for a spot to shoot his Western called *The Squaw Man*. He chose the varied landscape of Hollywood. Amid the orange groves, he changed a barn into a film studio.

Here in Hollywood, films could be shot in all seasons. The mild climate quickly appealed to other moviemakers. Through Hollywood magic, locations within 50 miles (80 km) of Los Angeles could be transformed into foreign lands. By the 1920s, Hollywood produced about 800 films per year.

Soon, the star system was born. At first, actors' names did not appear at the end of a movie. But, movie companies realized that films featuring well-known actors could earn more. Fan magazines helped turn actors such as Charlie Chaplin and Mary Pickford into the first million-dollar movie stars.

When television first became popular, Hollywood declared war on it. Television shows competed with movies for viewers. So, movie studios would not let their film stars perform on the small screen. But in the 1950s, Hollywood lifted the ban. Now, Los Angeles is known for its success in both industries.

Walt Disney shows plans for Disneyland's monorail. Built in 1959, it was the first monorail in America.

DISNEYLAND

In 1923, Kansas City cartoonist Walt Disney traveled to Hollywood. Soon, his cartoons were using the new technologies of sound and color. Disney became a producer with his own studio called Walt Disney Productions. His vision then grew into the original 107-acre (43-ha) Disneyland theme park in Anaheim, just outside Los Angeles. The grand opening was in 1955. Disneyland, Walt Disney once said, "will continue to grow as long as there is imagination left in the world." Today, his empire extends to Florida, France, and Japan.

Ocean breezes cool the coast of California during the summer. Inland, the San Fernando Valley heats up. Late summer brings hot, dry winds called Santa Anas. Warm winters bring rain but almost never snow. Most days in Los Angeles are sunny.

However, the city sometimes experiences natural disasters. In 1994, a powerful earthquake collapsed sections of major freeways and killed about 60 people. The earthquake registered 6.7 on the **Richter scale**.

The 1994 earthquake caused billions of dollars worth of damage to the Los Angeles area.

Smog hides Los Angeles's palm trees, skyscrapers, and mountains.

In 1993, high winds and dry air created brush fires. These fires destroyed more than 800 homes in the Los Angeles region. In 1998, El Niño created heavy rains and flooding, which caused sinkholes and mud slides. This weather event happens when the surface of the Pacific Ocean warms.

Some disasters are human-made. Cars crowding the highways give off exhaust pollution. This pollution mixes with sunlight to form a smoky fog called smog. The dirty air is kept in place by the surrounding mountains and is harmful to Angelenos' health.

Celebrating Cinco de Mayo on Olvera Street

Los Angeles is made up of **ethnically diverse** communities. Los Angeles County has the largest population of Hispanics, Native Americans, and Asians in the nation. Hispanics are the largest **minority** in the county.

Many ethnic neighborhoods are centered in downtown Los Angeles. This is where the original Spanish **pueblo** was built. The Olvera Street settlement and El Pueblo de Los Angeles Historic District remain important parts of the Los Angeles community.

Nearby are Chinatown and Little Tokyo. There are also pockets of Russian, Ethiopian, Armenian, and British **immigrants**. Many African Americans live in the Watts area.

The majority of Angelenos speak English. However, many television and radio programs are available in other languages.

Opposite Page: *Today, Olvera Street is a Mexican street market. Shoppers and diners are entertained by mariachis. Dancers perform for special events, such as Cinco de Mayo.*

Spanish language broadcasts are very common because of the growing Hispanic population. Other languages such as Japanese, Korean, and Arabic can be heard in the streets of Los Angeles.

Angelenos also practice a **diverse** number of religions. Christianity is the most common. But, many citizens practice Judaism, **Buddhism**, and **Islam**, as well as other newer religions.

Los Angeles schoolchildren at lunch

Children in California must attend school by age 6. But, some attend preschool when they are younger. Students are required to stay in school until age 18. However, some students leave school at age 16 or 17. To do this, they must graduate from high school or pass a special state exam.

Los Angeles County has hundreds of elementary, middle, and high schools. A few schools in the area focus on arts

At UCLA, students can study a wide range of subjects, including performing arts, law, and medicine.

education. The American artist Jackson Pollock attended Manual Arts High School. The world-renowned American Film Institute is also in L.A. Here, college students study the art of filmmaking.

Los Angeles County is filled with colleges and universities. The University of Southern California (USC) is one of the oldest universities in the area. It opened in 1880. The University of California Los Angeles (UCLA) was founded in 1919. And, the California State University has several branches in the region.

Rodeo Drive is found in the Beverly Hills neighborhood.

One popular activity in Los Angeles is stargazing, either in Hollywood or at Griffith Observatory. People can hike in Griffith Park, walk along Venice Beach, or shop on famous Rodeo Drive. And, visitors of all ages enjoy modern theme parks, such as Disneyland.

Sports are very popular with Angelenos. People dive, snorkel, surf, and water-ski. They skateboard, roller-skate, and play volleyball. In the mountains just outside the city, they can downhill ski. And, Angelenos watch professional sports teams.

Los Angeles is home to two baseball teams. The Los Angeles Dodgers play at Dodger Stadium. The California Angels play at Angel Stadium of Anaheim. Two basketball

The Staples Center opened in 1999.

teams are also based in Los Angeles. Both the L.A. Lakers and the L.A. Clippers shoot hoops at the Staples Center.

The city no longer has a professional football team. However, popular college football teams from UCLA and USC keep fans entertained. Two college teams also compete each year in the Tournament of Roses. On New Year's Day, the game kicks off at Rose Bowl Stadium after the Rose Parade.

SUMMER OLYMPICS

Los Angeles has hosted the Olympic Games twice. It first hosted the games in 1932. During that year's Summer Olympics, Babe Didrikson won two gold medals. She won one in the javelin throw and one in the hurdles. She earned a silver medal in the high jump because of her unusual style.

L.A. next hosted the Olympics in 1984. During these Summer Games, Carl Lewis won his first four gold medals. He matched Jesse Owens's 1936 success in the same four track-and-field events.

When in L.A., many tourists head to Hollywood. Here, they can take a tour of Warner Brothers Studios. Guides drive visitors around in golf carts. Sometimes, actors and crews can be spotted filming movies.

In 2002, Mike Myers received a star on the Hollywood Walk of Fame. More than 1,000 entertainers have been honored in this way.

There are more than 2,000 sidewalk stars on the Walk of Fame. Each star salutes a Hollywood legend. In front of Grauman's Chinese Theater, the hand- and footprints of famous actors grace the cement.

Stars of a different kind can be discovered at Griffith Observatory. This Los Angeles planetarium has a Zeiss star projector. It can show what space looks like on any date, including your birthday! Visitors can create their own earthquakes by jumping on the floor near the **seismograph**.

Santa Catalina Island was once a base for pirates and smugglers. People have lived on the island for more than 7,000 years. Yet, much of it is still in its natural state.

Tourists can investigate prehistoric life on Earth, too. Animals began falling into La Brea Tar Pits 40,000 years ago. Since 1906, scientists have fished out millions of fossils. Even more wildlife can be spotted on a trip to Santa Catalina Island.

Since 1542, Catalina has drawn visitors. Dolphins swim alongside boats. California gray whales **migrate** during the winter. And, flying fish can be lured above the waves with flashlights! From the magic of nature to the magic of Hollywood, Los Angeles is a city of amazing attractions.

GLOSSARY

Buddhism - a religion founded in India by Siddhartha Gautama. It teaches that pain and evil are caused by desire. If people have no desire, they will achieve a state of happiness called Nirvana.

cede - to grant or transfer something, usually by treaty.

commissioner - an official in charge of a government department.

culture - the customs, arts, and tools of a nation or people at a certain time.

diverse - composed of several distinct pieces or qualities.

economy - the way a nation uses its money, goods, and natural resources.

ethnic - of or having to do with a group of people who have the same race, nationality, or culture.

immigrate - to enter another country to live. A person who immigrates is called an immigrant.

Islam - the religion of Muslims. It is based on the teachings of Allah through the prophet Muhammad as they appear in the Koran.

migrate - to move from one place to another, often to find food.

minority - a racial, religious, or political group that is different from the larger group of which it is a part.

mission - a center or headquarters for religious work.

pueblo - typically a Native American village in the southwestern United States. It comes from the Spanish word for "village" or "people."

Richter scale - a scale invented by Charles F. Richter to measure the strength of earthquakes. The scale goes from about one to nine. A rating of one is a small earthquake, and a nine is a very damaging earthquake.

seismograph - a scientific instrument used to measure vibrations in the earth.

World War II - from 1939 to 1945, fought in Europe, Asia, and Africa. Great Britain, France, the United States, the Soviet Union, and their allies were on one side. Germany, Italy, Japan, and their allies were on the other side.

SAYING IT

Gaspar de Portolá - gahs-PAHR thay pawr-toh-LAH
Juan Crespi - KWAHN KRAYS-pee
Junípero Serra - hoo-NEE-puh-roh SEHR-uh
pueblo - PWEH-bloh
Richter scale - RIHK-tuhr SKAYL
Rodeo - ruh-DAY-oh
seismograph - SIZE-muh-graf

WEB SITES

To learn more about Los Angeles, visit ABDO Publishing Company on the World Wide Web at **www.abdopub.com**. Web sites about Los Angeles are featured on our Book Links page. These links are routinely monitored and updated to provide the most current information available.

INDEX

A
attractions 26, 27, 28, 29

C
Chaplin, Charlie 19
climate 18, 20, 21
Crespi, Juan 9

D
DeMille, Cecil B. 18

E
economy 16, 18
education 24, 25

G
government 12, 14, 15

H
Hahn, James K. 12
Hollywood 18, 19, 26, 28, 29

housing 12

I
immigrants 22

L
language 22, 23

M
Mexico 9, 10
mission 4, 8
motion picture industry 16, 18, 19, 25, 28

N
Native Americans 8, 9, 22
natural disasters 9, 20, 21, 28
Neve, Felipe de 9

P
Pickford, Mary 19
Pollock, Jackson 25
Portolá, Gaspar de 8, 9
pueblo 5, 9, 10, 22

R
religion 8, 23

S
San Diego 8
San Francisco 8
Serra, Junípero 8
Spain 4, 8, 9, 10, 22
sports 26, 27

T
transportation 4, 12, 14, 15

W
World War II 16